GRAPHIC LIBRARY™

GRAPHIC EXPEDITIONS

RESCUE IN THE BERMUDA TRIANGLE

AN Isabel Soto INVESTIGATION

by Marc Tyler Nobleman

illustrated by Joe Staton and Al Milgrom

Consultant:
Gian J. Quasar
Bermuda Triangle Researcher
www.bermuda-triangle.org

CAPSTONE PRESS
a capstone imprint

Graphic Library is published by Capstone Press,
151 Good Counsel Drive, P.O. Box 669, Mankato, Minnesota 56002.
www.capstonepub.com

 Books published by Capstone Press are manufactured with paper
containing at least 10 percent post-consumer waste.

Library of Congress Cataloging-in-Publication Data
Nobleman, Marc Tyler.
  Rescue in the Bermuda Triangle : an Isabel Soto investigation / by Marc Tyler Nobleman ;
illustrated by Joe Staton and Al Milgrom.
    p. cm.—(Graphic library, graphic expeditions)
  Includes bibliographical references and index.
  Summary: "In graphic novel format, follows the adventures of Isabel Soto as she explores
the mysteries of the Bermuda Triangle"—Provided by publisher.
  ISBN 978-1-4296-4770-0 (library binding)
  ISBN 978-1-4296-5633-7 (paperback)
  1. Bermuda Triangle—Juvenile literature. I. Staton, Joe. II. Milgrom, A. (Allen) III. Title.
IV. Series.

G558.N63 2011
001.94—dc22   2010000558

Designer
Alison Thiele

Media Researcher
Wanda Winch

Cover Artists
Tod G. Smith and Krista Ward

Production Specialist
Laura Manthe

Colorist
Michael Kelleher

Editor
Christopher L. Harbo

Photo credits:
Getty Images, Inc./Keystone, 9

Design elements:
Shutterstock/Chen Ping Hung (framed edge design); mmmm (world map design);
Mushakesa (abstract lines design); Najin (old parchment design)

TABLE OF CONTENTS

SIDES OF THE TRIANGLE

Official maps do not refer to the Bermuda Triangle. It is often described as an area in the Atlantic Ocean of at least 440,000 square miles (1,140,000 square kilometers). The triangle lies between Bermuda, Florida, and Puerto Rico.

However, the modern legend of the Bermuda Triangle began with Flight 19. On December 5, 1945, five U.S. Navy planes took off from Florida on a training mission.

Back then, pilots used compasses instead of GPS to navigate. At one point, Flight 19's flight leader radioed that they where lost. By evening, they had vanished.

Several planes were sent to find them. But one of those planes vanished too.

No wreckage from Flight 19 was ever found. Altogether, six planes and 27 men were gone.

AIR OF MYSTERY

In 1954, a Navy Super Constellation with 42 people aboard disappeared in the Bermuda Triangle. The plane left no trace. Making this disappearance more mysterious, much of the plane's cargo could float—including life rafts. The Navy admitted it could not determine what happened.

Some people believe that UFOs are responsible for Bermuda Triangle disappearances.

But we don't have evidence that aliens exist.

No scientific evidence, but this area is home to a high number of UFO sightings.

Hmm ... alien abductions might explain the lack of debris after many vanishings.

In 1971, the USS *John F. Kennedy* had problems with its communication equipment in the Bermuda Triangle. Crew members saw a glowing, soundless sphere hovering over their ship. The ship's radar screens glowed for 20 minutes. When they went back to normal, the sphere was gone.

ONE PIECE LEFT

In 1976, the large ship *Sylvia L. Ossa* went missing in the Bermuda Triangle. Unlike many other ships, she did leave something behind. Searchers found a wooden sign displaying the ship's name floating in the ocean.

In 1970, pilot Bruce Gernon coined the term electronic fog after an incident in the Bermuda Triangle. Gernon and two passengers flew into a huge cloud that changed into a tunnel.

Gernon said that the tunnel took him 100 miles, or 161 kilometers, away in only three minutes. Normally a trip that long would take 30 minutes.

Wait a minute. He claimed that he time traveled?

Or teleported. Some people believe that the Bermuda Triangle may contain portals through time and space.

BZZZT!

After seeing you travel, Isabel, I just might believe a Bermuda Triangle theory that weird.

Yes, I use portals. But unlike the Bermuda Triangle, the W.I.S.P. can be explained with science.

Speaking of the W.I.S.P. ...

This is the *Finders Keepers.* We just saw the *Downtown Dog!* We radioed the boat, but it didn't respond. Then it drifted into fog. I'm sending the coordinates.

That isn't far from here. Let's go.

Another theory is that the Bermuda Triangle is the site of the lost island of Atlantis.

Some people think that the ancient island left behind advanced technology or mystical powers that may be causing accidents.

You mean whatever caused Atlantis to sink might now be causing ships to sink? And planes to crash?

It's hard to find a shipwreck on the ocean floor. But a whole island should be easier to spot.

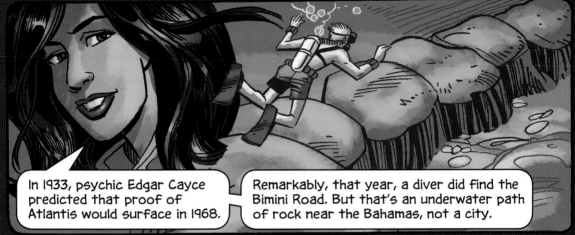

In 1933, psychic Edgar Cayce predicted that proof of Atlantis would surface in 1968.

Remarkably, that year, a diver did find the Bimini Road. But that's an underwater path of rock near the Bahamas, not a city.

Some people believe that the road was part of Atlantis.

But geologists say it's a natural formation. Either way, I don't believe rocks on the ocean floor can sink ships.

WHRRRRRR

What's that?

Pirates!

LEGENDARY ATLANTIS

According to legend, the island of Atlantis sank thousands of years ago in the Atlantic. The island was said to have a wealthy, highly advanced civilization that continued to live underwater after the island sank. However, no evidence has proven that Atlantis was real.

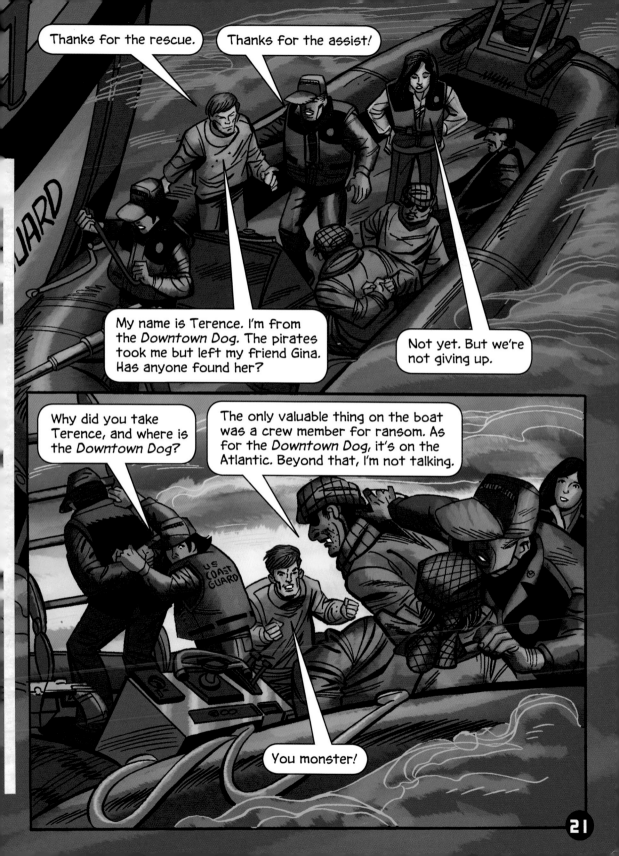

Yes. Terence radioed that we'd hit a storm, but there was no cause for panic. Soon after, pirates ambushed us and took him.

Did the pirates give you that bruise?

No. It happened after they were gone. It's hard to say.

Take your time.

I don't know much about boats, but I could tell the instruments had started to go haywire.

I looked up and saw a large weird glowing shape right over me.

Somehow, I wasn't afraid. I heard a boom. The boat rocked, and I hit my head. Next thing I remember, you two were standing over me.

Thank you for telling us. Let's get you to a hospital.

Later that morning. Coast Guard Headquarters, Miami
US COAST GUARD
Can you show me your list of missing vessels?
I'm sorry, Isabel. Given the Coast Guard's position on the Bermuda Triangle, we don't keep a list of missing vessels.
Let me try again. May I please see your list of overdue vessels?
Felipe, you can't pull one over on Isabel.
OVERDUE VESSELS
This report shows 150 overdue ships from the past year alone, with no explanations why.
Wow. I didn't think it was nearly that many!
Wow is right. I haven't officially changed my opinion. But I will admit the Bermuda Triangle has many unanswered questions.

This is one mystery we can't solve in a day. I've got to get back to New York to finish my other "lost" cause.

New York City

BEACH WEAR

I am not imagining it! A moment ago, that mannequin was wearing Bermuda shorts!

There you are, Mitzi! Lisa was worried sick. Time to get another overdue dog back home.

MORE ABOUT THE
BERMUDA TRIANGLE

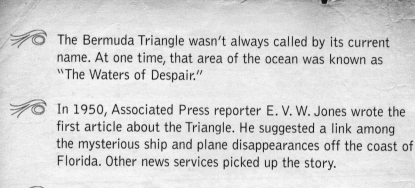

The Bermuda Triangle wasn't always called by its current name. At one time, that area of the ocean was known as "The Waters of Despair."

In 1950, Associated Press reporter E. V. W. Jones wrote the first article about the Triangle. He suggested a link among the mysterious ship and plane disappearances off the coast of Florida. Other news services picked up the story.

Lloyd's of London is a company that sells insurance. It claims that the Bermuda Triangle does not have more unexplained disappearances than other areas of ocean. Lloyd's also doesn't charge more money for insurance for craft traveling through the Bermuda Triangle.

The Bermuda Triangle's Puerto Rico Trench is the deepest part of the Atlantic Ocean. In places, the trench plunges 5.2 miles (8.4 kilometers) below the ocean's surface. Disappearances near the Puerto Rico Trench could explain why some accident wreckage is never found.

The USS *Cyclops'* disappearance remains the largest single noncombat loss of life in U.S. Navy history. Investigators filled 1,500 pages with details of the disappearance. But the cause of the incident remains a mystery.

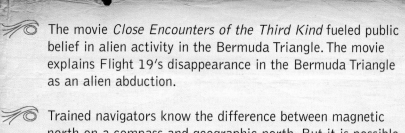

The movie *Close Encounters of the Third Kind* fueled public belief in alien activity in the Bermuda Triangle. The movie explains Flight 19's disappearance in the Bermuda Triangle as an alien abduction.

Trained navigators know the difference between magnetic north on a compass and geographic north. But it is possible that some navigators misread their compasses in the Bermuda Triangle. Doing so may have caused some accidents that became disappearances.

MORE ABOUT

NAME: Dr. Isabel "Izzy" Soto
DEGREES: History and Anthropology
BUILD: Athletic   **HAIR:** Dark Brown
EYES: Brown   **HEIGHT:** 5'7"

W.I.S.P.: The Worldwide Inter-dimensional Space/Time Portal developed by Max Axiom at Axiom Laboratory.

BACKSTORY: Dr. Isabel "Izzy" Soto caught the history bug as a little girl. Every night, her grandfather told her about his adventures exploring ancient ruins in South America. He believed lost cultures teach people a great deal about history.

Izzy's love of cultures followed her to college. She studied history and anthropology. On a research trip to Thailand, she discovered an ancient stone with mysterious energy. Izzy took the stone to Super Scientist Max Axiom who determined that the stone's energy cuts across space and time. Harnessing the power of the stone, he built a device called the W.I.S.P. It opens windows to any place and any time. Izzy now travels through time to see history unfold before her eyes. Although she must not change history, she can observe and investigate historical events.

bearings (BAYR-ingz)—your sense of direction in relation to where things are

coordinate (koh-OR-duh-nit)—one of a set of numbers used to show a position or a point on a line, graph, or map

debris (duh-BREE)—the scattered pieces of something that has been broken or destroyed

density (DEN-suh-tee)—how tightly the matter of an object is packed together

distress signal (di-STRES SIG-nuhl)—a call for help

geologist (jee-AHL-uh-jist)—someone who studies minerals, rocks, and soil

GPS (GEE PEE ESS)—an electronic tool used to find the location of an object; GPS stands for Global Positioning System

insurance (in-SHUR-uhnss)—a contract with a company that agrees to pay you in the event of sickness, fire, accident, or other loss

psychic (SYE-kik)—someone who claims to be able to tell what people are thinking or to predict the future

radar (RAY-dar)—a device that uses radio waves to track the location of objects

schooner (SKOO-nur)—a ship with masts at the front and back

supernatural (soo-pur-NACH-ur-uhl)—something that cannot be given an ordinary explanation

theory (THIHR-ee)—an idea that explains something that is unknown

vessel (VESS-uhl)—a boat or a ship

READ MORE

Belanger, Jeff. *The Mysteries of the Bermuda Triangle.* New York: Grosset & Dunlap, 2010.

DeMolay, Jack. *The Bermuda Triangle: The Disappearance of Flight 19.* Jr. Graphic Mysteries. New York: PowerKids Press, 2007.

Duffield, Katy S. *The Bermuda Triangle.* Mysterious Encounters. Detroit: KidHaven Press, 2008.

Miller, Connie Colwell. *The Bermuda Triangle: The Unsolved Mystery.* Mysteries of Science. Mankato, Minn.: Capstone Press, 2009.

Walker, Kathryn. *Mysteries of the Bermuda Triangle.* Unsolved! New York: Crabtree Publishing, 2009.

INTERNET SITES

FactHound offers a safe, fun way to find Internet sites related to this book. All of the sites on FactHound have been researched by our staff.

Here's all you do:

Visit *www.facthound.com*

Type in this code: 9781429647700

INDEX